Snežana Stefanović

Serbian:
Simple Sentences 1

In Latin and Cyrillic script
with English translation

Level: A1 – Beginners

www.serbian-reader.com.

FOREWORD

The book „Serbian: Simple Sentences 1", language level A1 (beginners) offers ready-made sentences for learning Serbian. The sentences are designed for language level A1 – beginners and grouped into common topics for everyday language use. All sentences are written in the present tense and the texts are written in both Latin and Cyrillic alphabet. For each sentence there is also a translation into English.

More information on the Internet at: www.serbian-reader.com

CONTENT – SADRŽAJ

Simple sentences in Latin script

1. Getting to know each other I – Upoznavanje I
2. Getting to know each other II – Upoznavanje II
3. What is your name? – Kako se zoveš?
4. In the city – U gradu
5. In the café – U kafiću
6. In the restaurant – U restoranu
7. How do the dishes taste? – Kakva su jela?
8. At the vegetable market – Na pijaci
9. Leisure – Slobodno vreme
10. Personal description – Opis osobe
11. Apartment description – Opis stana
12. In the evening – Uveče
13. Everyday life – Svakodnevica
14. My job – Moj posao

Simple Sentences in Cyrillic script

1. Getting to know each other I – Упознавање I
2. Getting to know each other II – Упознавање II
3. What is your name? – Како се зовеш?
4. In the city – У граду
5. In the café – У кафићу
6. In the restaurant – У ресторану
7. How do the dishes taste? – Каква су јела?
8. At the vegetable market – На пијаци
9. Leisure – Слободно време
10. Personal description – Опис особе
11. Apartment description – Опис стана
12. In the evening – Увече
13. Everyday life – Свакодневица
14. My job – Мој посао

Serbian simple sentences in Latin script

1. Getting to know each other I – Upoznavanje I

Dobar dan!	Hello! Good day!
Kako si?	How are you?
Hvala, dobro. A ti?	Fine, thanks. And you?
I ja sam dobro.	I´m fine, too.
Kako je tvoj muž?	How´s your husband?
Hvala, on je dobro.	He´s fine, thanks.
Kako je tvoja žena?	How´s your wife?
Ona je tako–tako.	She´s so-so.
Odakle si?	Where are you from?
Ja sam iz Beograda. A ti?	I come from Belgrade. And where are you from?
Ja sam iz Berlina.	I come from Berlin.
Odakle je tvoja drugarica?	Where´s your girlfriend from?

Ona je iz Berna.	She comes from Bern.
Odakle je tvoj drug?	Where is your friend from?
On je iz Švajcarske.	He comes from Switzerland.
Odakle iz Švajcarske?	Where from Switzerland?
Iz Ženeve.	From Geneva.

2. Getting to know each other II – Upoznavanje II

Dobro jutro!	Good morning!
Kako se kaže: „excellent"?	How do you say: „excellent"?
Kaže se: „odlično".	I say (One says): „odlično".
Šta znači: „loše"?	What does „loše" mean?
„Loše" znači „bad".	„Loše" means „bad".
Jesi ti loše?	Do you feel bad?
Ne, ja sam odlično.	No, I am excellent.
Šta si po zanimanju?	What is your profession?

Interesantno.	Interesting.
Ja sam službenik po zanimanju.	I´m an employee by profession.
Šta su tvoji roditelji po zanimanju?	What do your parents do?
Moja majka je penzionerka.	My mother is a pensioner.
Moj otac je u penziji.	My father is retired.

3. What´s your name? – Kako se zoveš?

Dobro veče!	Good evening!
Kako se zove tvoj brat?	What is your brother´s name?
Moj brat se zove Ognjen.	My brother´s name is Ognjen.
Kako se zove tvoja sestra?	What´s your sister´s name?
Moja sestra se zove Biljana.	My sister´s name is Biljana.
Ne razumem.	I don´t understand.
Polako, polako!	Slow down, slow down!

Ne znam.	I don´t know.
Ide.	It works. It goes.
Samo malo.	Just a little bit. / Just a moment.
Vidimo se!	See you!
Doviđenja!	Goodbye!
Do sutra!	See you tomorrow!

4. In the city – U gradu

Izvinite, možete da mi pomognete?	Excuse me, can you help me?
Molim vas, gde je ovde parkiralište?	Please, where´s the parking lot?
Razumem.	I see.
Izvinite, gde je ovde apoteka?	Excuse me, where´s the pharmacy?
Tu, u blizini.	It´s nearby.
Izvinite, gde je ovde bolnica?	Excuse me, where´s the hospital?
Odmah ovde.	It´s right here.

Daleko.	It´s far away.
Izvinite, gde je ovde pozorište „Atelje 212“?	Excuse me, where´s the theater „Atelje 212“?
Iza ćoška.	Around the corner.
Izvinite, gde je ovde tramvajska stanica?	Excuse me, where´s the tramway station?
Tamo.	There.
Izvinite, gde je ovde pošta?	Excuse me, where´s the post office?
Idite samo pravo.	Just go straight ahead.
Izvinite, gde je ovde policijska stanica?	Excuse me, where is the police station?
Idite levo, pa desno.	Go left, then right.
Mi tražimo bioskop „Fontana“.	We´re looking for the „Fontana“ cinema.
Idite desno, pa levo, pa desno.	Go right, then left, then right.
Gde je ovde lift?	Where´s the lift?
Idite uvek desno.	Go right only.
Gde je ovde pijaca „Banovo brdo“?	Where is the vegetable market „Banovo brdo?“
Vidite onu ulicu tamo? Da, tamo je.	So you see that street there? Yes, there it is.

Gde je ovde bankomat?	Where´s an ATM (cash mashine) here?
Tamo preko.	Over there.
Gde je ovde izlaz?	Where´s the exit?
Levo.	To the left.
Gde je ovde knjižara?	Where is the bookstore here?
Desno.	On the right.
Mnogo hvala.	Thanks a lot.
Nema na čemu.	You´re welcome.
Doviđenja!	Goodbye!

5. In the café – U kafiću

Dobar dan!	Hello!
Izvinite, možemo da naručimo?	Excuse me, can we place an order?
Ja želim kafu i običnu vodu.	I would like a coffee and tap water with it.

Molim vas s mlekom.	With milk, please.
Molim vas bez mleka.	Without milk, please.
Ja želim duplu kafu.	I´d like a double coffee.
Mi želimo dve kafe.	We would like 2 coffees.
Ja želim samo espreso.	I only want an espresso.
Kakve imate čajeve?	What kind of tea do you have?
Molim vas bez limuna.	Please, without lemon.
Ja želim samo vodu.	I only want water.
Ja želim pola litre vode.	I want half a liter of water.
Imate li negaziranu vodu?	Da you have still water?
Da, molim.	Yes, please.
Molim bez leda.	Without ice cubes, please.
Ja želim pivo.	I want a beer.
Kakva piva imate?	What kind of beer do you have?
Ja želim pivo u boci.	I´d like a bottled beer.

Ja želim točeno pivo.	I want beer on tap.
Je li pivo hladno?	Is the beer cold?
Ja želim rakiju.	I want a schnapps.
Koju rakiju mi preporučujete?	What schnapps do you recommend?
Ja želim da probam domaću vrstu rakije.	I want to taste a local kind of schnapps.
Ja želim čašu vina.	I want a glass of wine.
Imate li crno vino?	Do you have red wine?
Imate li belo vino?	Do you have white wine?
Imate li neko dobro domaće vino?	Do you have a good local wine?
Ko proizvodi to vino?	Whe makes the wine?
Izvinite, gde je ovde toalet?	Excuse me, where is the toilet?
Imate li i bežični pristup internetu (WLAN)?	Do you have WLAN here also?
Kako glasi lozinka za bežični pristup internetu (WLAN)?	What is he password for WLAN?
To je sve, hvala.	That is all, thank you.
Mi želimo da platimo.	We would like to pay.

Doviđenja!	Goodbye!

6. In the restaurant – U restoranu

Molim vas, gde je naš sto?	Where is our table, please?
Gde je moje mesto?	Where is my seat?
Možemo li da dobijemo jelovnik?	Can we get the menu?
Šta možete da nam preporučite?	What can you recommend us?
Imate li vinsku kartu?	Do you have a wine list?
Imate li danas dnevni meni?	Do you have the menu of the day?
Hoćemo da naručimo predjelo?	Do you want to order an appetizer?
Možemo da uzmemo hladno predjelo.	We will have a cold starter.
Ja želim toplo predjelo.	I will have a warm starter.
Mi smo veoma gladni.	Wa are very hungry.
Mi nismo jako gladni.	We are not very hungry.
Šta možemo da uzmemo za glavno jelo?	What should we take as our main course?

Ja ne jedem meso.	I don´t eat meat.
Mi želimo nešto lagano.	We want something light.
Možete da nam stavite ovo jelo na dva tanjira?	Can you split this dish into two plates?
U jelovniku stoji: „domaća supa". Šta je to?	The menu says: „domaća supa". What is that?
Šta je uz ovo jelo prilog?	What is the side dish with this dish?
Mogu li da dobijem ovo jelo bez priloga?	Can I get this dish without a side dish?
Je li to slatko ili slano?	Is it sweet or salty?
Ja ne poznajem to jelo.	I don´t know this food.
Recite mi – kakvo je ovo jelo?	Tell me – what is this food like?
Imate li neki srpski specijalitet?	Do you have a Serbian speciality?
Zašto ne?	Why not?
Ipak ne.	Not really.
Onda ćemo da probamo to jelo.	Then let´s try this dish.
Mi želimo i desert.	We also want a dessert.
Mi želimo dve čaše vina.	We want 2 glasses of wine.

Molim vas i pola litre negazirane vode.	Please also half a liter of still water.
Molim vas samo običnu vodu.	Please only tap water.
Mi obično pijemo kafu posle.	We drink coffee afterwards.
Molim vas novu kašiku.	Can I get a new spoon?
Mogu li da dobijem novu viljušku?	Can I get a new fork?
Imate li pepeljaru?	Do you have an ashtray?
Mogu li da dobijem još jednu salvetu?	Can I get another napkin?
Da, to je veoma ukusno.	Yes, it tastes good.
Da, mi smo veoma zadovoljni.	Yes, we are very pleased.
Ne, mi nismo zadovoljni.	No, we are not satisfied.
Nažalost.	Unfortunately.
Molim vas, možemo da platimo?	Please, can we pay?
Račun, molim.	Bill, please.
Mnogo hvala.	Thank you very much.

7. How do the dishes taste? – Kakva su jela?

Kakav je doručak?	How is the breakfast?
Doručak je veoma ukusan.	The breakfast is very tasty.
Je li hleb svež?	Is the bread fresh?
Da, hleb je svež.	Yes, the bread is fresh.
Je li čaj topao?	Is the tea warm?
Ne, čaj je hladan.	No, the tea is cold.
Salata uopšte nije slana.	The salad is not salted at all.
Supa je bljutava.	The soup is bland.
Ovaj odrezak nije pečen.	The schnitzel is not fried.
Ovaj kolač je sladak.	This cake is sweet.
Vaša predjela su veoma izdašna.	Your appetizers are very rich.
Glavno jelo nije jeftino.	The main course is not cheap.
Sos je nažalost kiseo.	Unfortunately, the sauce is sour.

Piletina je prezačinjena.	The chicken is too spicy.
Meso je odlično pečeno.	The meat is excellent fried.
Ova svinjetina nije dobra.	This pork is not good.
Riba je lagano jelo.	Fish is a light meal.
Krastavac je gorak.	The cucumber is bitter.
Kakva je večera?	How is the dinner?
Ja želim nešto toplo.	I want something warm.
Ja želim krepku supu.	I want a strong soup.
Ja želim svežu salatu i malo domaćeg sira.	I want a fresh salad and some homemade cheese.
Mi želimo samo svežu salatu.	We only want a fresh salad.
Sladoled je topao.	The ice cream is warm.
Vaši deserti izgledaju veoma dobro.	Your desserts look very good.

8. At the vegetable market – Na pijaci

Molim vas, koliko ovo košta?	Please, how much does it cost?
To je veoma jeftino.	That´s very cheap.
To je veoma skupo.	That´s very expensive.
Odakle dolazi ovo voće?	Where does the fruit come from?
Odakle dolazi ovo povrće?	Where do the vegetables come from?
Je li voće sveže?	Is the fruit fresh?
Je li povrće sveže?	Are the vegetables fresh?
Ja želim jedan kilogram.	I want one kilogram.
Ja želim pola kilograma.	I want half a kilogram.
Ja želim dva kilograma.	I want 2 kilograms.
Ja želim samo jedno pakovanje voća.	I only want one box of fruit.
Mogu li da izaberem voće?	Can I choose the fruit by myself?
To je previše.	This is too much.

To je premalo.	This is too little.
Ta jabuka je trula.	This apple is rotten.
Ne, hvala lepa.	No, thank you very much.
Voće je za kolač.	The fruit is for a cake.
Povrće je za supu.	The vegetables are for a soup.
Molim vas samo velike komade.	Only big pieces, please.
Molim vas samo male komade.	Only small pieces, please.
Mogu li da dobijem samo pola?	Can I only get half?
Ja nemam kesicu.	I don´t have a bag.
Ja nemam sitniš.	I have no change.

9. Leisure – Slobodno vreme

Šta radiš u slobodno vreme?	What do you do in your leisure?
Imaš li mnogo slobodnog vremena?	Do you have much leisure?
Imaš li hobi?	Do you have a hobby?
Koji je tvoj hobi?	What kind of hobby do you have?
Da li voliš fudbal?	Do you like soccer?
Da li igraš košarku?	Do you play basketball?
Moj hobi je kuvanje.	My hobby is cooking.
Moji hobiji su knjige i čitanje.	My hobbies are books and reading.
Moj hobi je sviranje.	My hobby is playing music.
Ja sviram klavir i gitaru.	I play piano and guitar.
Ja volim duge šetnje.	I like long walks.
Ja volim prirodu.	I like nature.
Moj hobi je planinarenje.	My hobby is mountain climbing.

Moj hobi je gledanje filmova.	My hobby is watching movies.
Kako često se baviš tvojim hobijem?	How often do you deal with your hobby?
Svaki dan.	Every day.
Svaki vikend.	Every weekend.
Ne često, samo ponekad.	Not often, just sometimes.
Imaš li vremena za to?	Do you have time for that?
Ne uvek.	Not always.
Za hobi imam uvek vremena.	I always have time for a hobby.
Voliš da ideš u bioskop?	Do you like going to the movies?
Voliš operu?	Do you like the opera?
Kada imam vremena, ja ostajem kod kuće.	When I have time, I stay at home.
Ja volim da gledam televiziju.	I like watching TV.
Ja rado slikam i crtam.	I like painting and drawing.
Moj hobi je joga.	My hobby is yoga.
Moj hobi je skijanje.	My hobby is skiing.

Moj hobi je hokej.	My hobby is ice hockey.
Moj hobi je plivanje.	My hobby is swimming.
Ja idem svaki vikend da plivam na bazen.	I go to the swimming pool every weekend.
Moj hobi su putovanja.	My hobby is travelling.
Ja volim da posećujem gradove.	I like to visit cities.
Ja volim da posećujem daleke zemlje.	I like to visit distant countries.
Ja se bavim sportom.	I do sports.
Kojim sportom se baviš?	What kind of sport do you do?
Ja se bavim odbojkom.	I play volleyball.
Ja igram stolni tenis.	I play table tennis.
Ja nemam hobi.	I have no hobby.

10. Personal description – Opis osobe

Kako izgleda tvoja drugarica?	What does your girlfriend look like?
Ona je niska i ima smeđu kosu.	She is small and has brown hair.
Kako izgleda tvoj drug?	What does your friend look like?
On je visok i ima plavu kosu.	He is tall and has blond hair.
Šta on nosi?	What does he wear?
On nosi pantalone i košulju.	He wears pants and a shirt.
Ona nosi uvek suknje i bluze.	She always wears skirts and blouses.
Kakav je njegov karakter?	What is his character like?
On je simpatičan i drag.	He is sympathetic and kind.
Ona je moderna i interesantna.	She is modern and interesting.
On je veoma glasan.	He is very loud.
Ona je vesela.	She is cheerful.
Moj kolega je sada veoma ljut.	My colleague is very angry now.

Zašto je tvoj kolega ljut?	Why is your colleague angry?
Njegova jakna je prljava.	His jacket is dirty.
Moja koleginica je tužna.	My colleague is sad.
Zašto je tvoja koleginica tužna?	Why is your colleague sad?
Njena suknja je prljava.	Her skirt is dirty.
Kakav je tvoj pas?	What does your dog look like?
On je mali, mlad i brz.	It´s small, young and fast.
Kakva je tvoja mačka?	What does your cat look like?
Ona je debela i spora.	It´s fat and slow.
Kakva je tvoja tašna?	What does your bag look like?
Ona je velika i skupa.	It´s big and expensive.
Ona je loše jer je žedna.	She´s feeling bad because she´s thirsty.
Kakva je njegova košulja?	What does his shirt look like?
Kakva je njena suknja?	What does her skirt look like?
Kakav je njegov kaput?	What does his coat look like?

| Moja koža je tamna, zar ne? | My skin is tanned, isn´t it? |
| On je loše jer je gladan. | He´s feeling bad because he´s hungry. |

11. Apartment description – Opis stana

O, kako je vaš stan velik!	Oh, how big is your apartement!
Je li vaš stan skup?	Is your apartment expensive?
Stan je ogroman, ali nije skup.	The apartment is huge, but not expensive.
Vi imate sreće sa stanom.	You are lucky with the apartment.
Vaša terasa je prostrana.	Your terrace is spacious.
Dnevna soba je moderna i ugodna.	The living room is modern and comfortable
Spavaća soba je minijaturna.	The bedroom is tiny.
Ovde primate goste, zar ne?	This is where you receive the guests, isn´t it?
Naš balkon je mali, ali lep.	Our balcony is small but beautiful.
Imate i trpezariju?	Do you have a dining room also?
Ne, nažalost nemamo trpezariju.	No, unfortunately we do not have a dining room.
Naše kupatilo je jednostavno i praktično.	Our bathroom is simple and practical.
Njihov toalet je mali, ali čist i lep.	Your toilet is small but clean and beautiful.

Je li vaš stan topao?	Is your apartment warm?
O da, stan je veoma topao.	Oh yes, the apartment is very warm.
Da li imate ostavu?	Do you have a storage room?
Ne, nažalost nemamo ostavu.	No, unfortunately, we don´t have a storage room.
Kakav je soliter?	What is the building like?
Soliter je star, ali lep.	The building is old, but beautiful.
Kakav je lift?	What is the lift like?
Lift radi.	The lift is in use.
Mi nemamo lift.	We don´t have an elevator.
Kakva je ulica?	What is the street like?
Ulica je dugačka i glasna.	The street is long and loud.

12. In the evening – Uveče

Kuda idemo večeras?	Where are we going tonight?
Večeras idemo na večeru.	Tonight, we are going to dinner.

Kuda idemo u subotu?	Where are we going on Saturday?
U subotu idemo u grad.	On Saturday we are going in the town.
Kuda tačno?	Where exactly?
Idemo da večeramo u restoran.	We are going to the restaurant for dinner.
Kuda idemo posle?	Where are we going afterwards?
Posle idemo u kafanu.	Afterwards we will go to a coffee house.
Šta slavimo u subotu?	What are we celebrating on Saturday?
U subotu slavimo rođendan.	On Saturday we celebrate my birthday.
Kada se vidimo?	When will I see you?
Vidimo se u pola osam.	See you at 7:30 pm.
Kuda ideš sutra?	Where are you going tomorrow?
Sutra idem u pozorište.	Tomorrow I´m going to the theatre.
Kuda ideš sutra uveče?	Where are you going tomorrow night?
Sutra uveče ne idem nikuda.	I´m not going anywhere tomorrow night.
Kuda ideš prekosutra?	Where are you going the day after tomorrow?

Prekosutra imam sastanak s Lelom.	The day after tomorrow I have a date with Lela.
Oko koliko časova se vidimo?	At what time will I see you?
Vidimo se oko pet.	See you around 5 o´clock.

| Do kada ostajemo u klubu? | Until when do we stay at the club? |
| Do ponoći. | Until midnight. |

Šta želiš da radiš sutra uveče?	What do you want to do tomorrow in the evening?
Sutra uveče želim da gledam televiziju.	Tomorrow in the evening I want to watch TV.
Kuda želiš da ideš u petak uveče?	Where do you want to go on Friday evening?
U petak uveče želim da idem na izložbu.	On Friday evening I want to go to the exhibition.
Kuda idemo u nedelju uveče?	Where do we want to go on Sunday evening?
U nedelju uveče idemo u operu.	On Sunday evening we are going to the opera.

13. Everyday life – Svakodnevica

| Kada se budiš? | When do you wake up? |
| Ja se budim svaki dan oko sedam. | I wake up around 7 o´clock every day. |

Šta doručkuješ?	What do you eat for breakfast?
Volim lagan doručak.	I like a light breakfast.
Ja ne doručkujem.	I don´t eat breakfast.
Ja volim ujutro mnogo da jedem.	I like to eat a lot in the morning.
Šta radiš prepodne?	What do you do in the morning?
Prepodne radim.	I work in the morning.
Prepodne sam na poslu.	In the morning, I´m at work.
Kada ručaš?	When do you eat lunch?
Obično ručam oko dvanaest.	I usually have lunch around noon.
Šta obično ručaš?	What do you usually eat for lunch?
Ja jedem u kantini.	I eat in the canteen.
Ja jedem kod kuće.	I eat at home.
Ja kuvam kod kuće svaki dan.	I cook at home every day.
Ja ne ručam jer kasno doručkujem.	I don´t eat lunch because I have a late breakfast.

Šta radiš poslepodne?	What do you do in the afternoon?
Poslepodne sam na poslu.	In the afternoon I am at work.
Poslepodne sam kod kuće s decom.	In the afternoon I am at home with the children.
Poslepodne se odmaram.	In the afternoon I rest.
Da li se dugo odmaraš?	Do you rest long?
Ja se kratko odmaram.	I rest a little.
Ja se ne odmaram jer nemam vremena.	I don´t rest because I don´t have time.
Šta radiš uveče?	What do you do in the evening?
Uveče gledam televiziju.	In the evening I watch TV.
Uveče čitam novine.	I the evening I read the paper.
Uveče čitam knjige.	In the evening I read books.
Uveče spremam stan.	In the evening I tidy the apartment.
Uveče sam s decom.	In the evening I am with the children.
Kada ideš da spavaš?	When do you go to bed?

Obično idem kasno da spavam.	I usually go to bed late.
Obično idem rano da spavam.	I usually go to bed early.

14. My job – Moj posao

Gde radiš?	Where do you work?
Šta si po zanimanju?	What is your profession?
Kakav je tvoj posao?	What is your job like?
Moj posao je interesantan i ugodan.	My job is interesting and pleasant.
Moj posao je naporan i težak.	My job is exhausting and difficult.
Moj posao je lagan i jednostavan.	My job is easy and simple.
Imaš li šefa?	Do you have a boss?
Moj šef je veoma ugodan.	My boss is very pleasant.
Ja nemam šefa, ja radim samostalno.	I don´t have a boss, I am self-employed.
Moji saradnici na poslu su simpatični.	My colleagues at work are likeable.

Ja radim od devet do pet.	I work from 9 to 5.
Ponekad radim prekovremeno.	I work overtime sometimes.
Kako ideš na posao?	How do you get to work?
Idem peške jer je moj biro blizu.	I walk becuase my office is close by.
Ja ne želim da menjam posao.	I don´t want to change my job.
Ja volim moj posao jer je zabavan.	I like my job because it is entertaining.
Jesi sada na bolovanju?	Are you on sick leave now?
Da, imam gripu.	Yes, I have a flu.
Danas trebam da završim posao.	Today I am supposed to finish my work.
Imam mnogo posla.	I have a lot to do.
Imam malo posla.	I have little to do.

Simple sentences in Cyrillic script

1. Getting to know each other I – Упознавање I

Добар дан!	Hello! Good day!
Како си?	How are you?
Хвала, добро. А ти?	Fine, thanks. And you?
И ја сам добро.	I´m fine, too.
Како је твој муж?	How´s your husband?
Хвала, он је добро.	He´s fine, thanks.
Како је твоја жена?	How´s your wife?
Она је тако-тако.	She´s so-so.
Одакле си?	Where are you from?
Ја сам из Београда. А ти?	I come from Belgrade. And where are you from?
Ја сам из Берлина.	I come from Berlin.
Одакле је твоја другарица?	Where´s your girlfriend from?

Она је из Берна.	She comes from Bern.
Одакле је твој друг?	Where is your friend from?
Он је из Швајцарске.	He comes from Switzerland.
Одакле из Швајцарске?	Where from Switzerland?
Из Женеве.	From Geneva.

2. Getting to know each other I – Упознавање II

Добро јутро!	Good morning!
Како се каже: „ausgezeichnet“?	How do you say: „excellent“?
Каже се: „одлично“.	I say (One says): „odlično“.
Шта значи: „лоше“?	What does „loše“ mean?
„Лоше“ значи „schlecht“.	„Loše“ means „bad“.
Јеси ти лоше?	Do you feel bad?
Не, ја сам одлично.	No, I am excellent.
Шта си по занимању?	What is your profession?

Интересантно.	Interesting.
Ја сам службеник по занимању.	I´m an employee by profession.
Шта су твоји родитељи по занимању?	What do your parents do?
Моја мајка је пензионерка.	My mother is a pensioner.
Мој отац је у пензији.	My father is retired.

3. What is your name? – Како се зовеш?

Добро вечс!	Good evening!
Како се зове твој брат?	What is your brother´s name?
Мој брат се зове Огњен.	My brother´s name is Ognjen.
Како се зове твоја сестра?	What´s your sister´s name?
Моја сестра се зове Биљана.	My sister´s name is Biljana.
Не разумем.	I don´t understand.
Полако, полако!	Slow down, slow down!
Не знам.	I don´t know.

Иде.	It works. It goes.
Само мало.	Just a little bit. / Just a moment.
Видимо се!	See you!
Довиђења!	Goodbye!
До сутра!	See you tomorrow!

4. In the city – У граду

Извините, можете да ми помогнете?	Excuse me, can you help me?
Молим вас, где је овде паркиралиште?	Please, where´s the parking lot?
Разумем.	I see.
Извините, где је овде апотека?	Excuse me, where´s the pharmacy?
Ту, у близини.	It´s nearby.
Извините, где је овде болница?	Excuse me, where´s the hospital?
Одмах овде.	It´s right here.
Далеко.	It´s far away.

Извините, где је овде позориште "Атеље 212"?	Excuse me, where´s the theater „Atelje 212"?
Иза ћошка.	Around the corner.
Извините, где је овде трамвајска станица?	Excuse me, where´s the tramway station?
Тамо.	There.
Извините, где је овде пошта?	Excuse me, where´s the post office?
Идите само право.	Just go straight ahead.
Извините, где је овде полицијска станица?	Excuse me, where is the police station?
Идите лево па десно.	Go left, then right.
Ми тражимо биоскоп "Фонтана".	We´re looking for the „Fontana" cinema.
Идите десно па лево па десно.	Go right, then left, then right.
Где је овде лифт?	Where´s the lift?
Идите увек десно.	Go right only.
Где је овде пијаца „Баново брдо"?	Where is the vegetable market „Banovo brdo?"
Видите ону улицу тамо? Да, тамо је.	So you see that street there? Yes, there it is.
Где је овде банкомат?	Where´s an ATM (cash mashine) here?

Тамо преко.	Over there.
Где је овде излаз?	Where´s the exit?
Лево.	To the left.
Где је овде књижара?	Where is the bookstore here?
Десно.	On the right.
Много хвала.	Thanks a lot.
Нема на чему.	You´re welcome.
Довиђења!	Goodbye!

5. In the café – У кафићу

Добар дан!	Hello!
Извините, можемо да наручимо?	Excuse me, can we place an order?
Ја желим кафу и обичну воду.	I would like a coffee and tap water with it.

Молим вас с млеком.	With milk, please.
Молим вас без млека.	Without milk, please.
Ја желим дуплу кафу.	I´d like a double coffee.
Ми желимо две кафе.	We would like 2 coffees.
Ја желим само еспресо.	I only want an espresso.
Какве имате чајеве?	What kind of tea do you have?
Молим вас без лимуна.	Please, without lemon.
Ја желим само воду.	I only want water.
Ја желим пола литре воде.	I want half a liter of water.
Имате ли негазирану воду?	Da you have still water?
Да, молим.	Yes, please.

Молим без леда.	Without ice cubes, please.
Ја желим пиво.	I want a beer.
Каква пива имате?	What kind of beer do you have?
Ја желим пиво у боци.	I´d like a bottled beer.
Ја желим точено пиво.	I want beer on tap.
Је ли пиво хладно?	Is the beer cold?
Ја желим ракију.	I want a schnapps.
Коју ракију ми препоручујете?	What schnapps do you recommend?
Ја желим да пробам домаћу врсту ракије.	I want to taste a local kind of schnapps.
Ја желиим чашу вина.	I want a glass of wine.
Имате ли црно вино?	Do you have red wine?

Имате ли бело вино?	Do you have white wine?
Имате ли неко добро домаће вино?	Do you have a good local wine?
Ко производи то вино?	Whe makes the wine?
Извините, где је овде тоалет?	Excuse me, where is the toilet?
Имате ли и бежични приступ интернету (WLAN)?	Do you have WLAN here also?
Како гласи лозинка за бежични приступ интернету (WLAN)?	What is he password for WLAN?
То је све, хвала.	That is all, thank you.
Ми желимо да платимо.	We would like to pay.
Довиђења!	Goodbye!

6. In the restaurant – У ресторану

Молим вас, где је наш сто?	Where is our table, please?
Где је моје место?	Where is my seat?
Можемо ли да добијемо јеловник?	Can we get the menu?
Шта можете да нам препоручите?	What can you recommend us?
Имате ли винску карту?	Do you have a wine list?
Имате ли данас дневни мени?	Do you have the menu of the day?
Хоћемо да наручимо предјело?	Do you want to order an appetizer?
Можемо да узмемо хладно предјело.	We will have a cold starter.
Ја желим топло предјело.	I will have a warm starter.
Ми смо веома гладни.	Wa are very hungry.
Ми нисмо јако гладни.	We are not very hungry.
Шта можемо да узмемо за главно јело?	What should we take as our main course?
Ја не једем месо.	I don´t eat meat.

Ми желимо нешто лагано.	We want something light.
Можете да нам ставите ово јело на два тањира?	Can you split this dish into two plates?
У јеловнику стоји: „домаћа супа". Шта је то?	The menu says: „domaća supa". What is that?
Шта је уз ово јело прилог?	What is the side dish with this dish?
Могу ли да добијем ово јело без прилога?	Can I get this dish without a side dish?
Је ли то слатко или слано?	Is it sweet or salty?
Ја не познајем то јело.	I don´t know this food.
Реците ми – какво је ово јело?	Tell me – what is this food like?
Имате ли неки српски специјалитет?	Do you have a Serbian speciality?
Зашто не?	Why not?
Ипак не.	Not really.
Онда ћемо да пробамо то јело.	Then let´s try this dish.
Ми желимо и десерт.	We also want a dessert.
Ми желимо две чаше вина.	We want 2 glasses of wine.
Молим вас и пола литре негазиране воде.	Please also half a liter of still water.

Молим вас само обичну воду.	Please only tap water.
Ми обично пијемо кафу после.	We drink coffee afterwards.
Молим вас нову кашику.	Can I get a new spoon?
Могу ли да добијем нову виљушку?	Can I get a new fork?
Имате ли пепељару?	Do you have an ashtray?
Могу ли да добијем још једну салвету?	Can I get another napkin?
Да, то је веома укусно.	Yes, it tastes good.
Да, ми смо веома задовољни.	Yes, we are very pleased.
Не, ми нисмо задовољни.	No, we are not satisfied.
Нажалост.	Unfortunately.
Молим вас, можемо да платимо?	Please, can we pay?
Рачун молим.	Bill, please.
Много хвала.	Thank you very much.

7. How do the dishes taste? – Каква су јела?

Какав је доручак?	How is the breakfast?
Доручак је веома укусан.	The breakfast is very tasty.
Је ли хлеб свеж?	Is the bread fresh?
Да, хлеб је свеж.	Yes, the bread is fresh.
Је ли чај топао?	Is the tea warm?
Не, чај је хладан.	No, the tea is cold.
Салата уопште није слана.	The salad is not salted at all.
Супа је бљутава.	The soup is bland.
Овај одрезак није печен.	The schnitzel is not fried.
Овај колач је сладак.	This cake is sweet.
Ваша предјела су веома издашна.	Your appetizers are very rich.
Главно јело није јефтино.	The main course is not cheap.
Сос је нажалост кисео.	Unfortunately, the sauce is sour.

Пилетина је презачињена.	The chicken is too spicy.
Месо је одлично печено.	The meat is excellent fried.
Ова свињетина није добра.	This pork is not good.
Риба је лагано јело.	Fish is a light meal.
Краставац је горак.	The cucumber is bitter.
Каква је вечера?	How is the dinner?
Ја желим нешто топло.	I want something warm.
Ја желим крепку супу.	I want a strong soup.
Ја желим свежу салату и мало домаћег сира.	I want a fresh salad and some homemade cheese.
Ми желимо само свежу салату.	We only want a fresh salad.
Сладолед је топао.	The ice cream is warm.
Ваши десерти изгледају веома добро.	Your desserts look very good.

8. At the vegetable market – На пијаци

Молим вас, колико ово кошта?	Please, how much does it cost?
То је веома јефтино.	That´s very cheap.

То је веома скупо.	That´s very expensive.
Одакле долази ово воће?	Where does the fruit come from?
Одакле долази ово поврће?	Where do the vegetables come from?
Је ли воће свеже?	Is the fruit fresh?
Је ли поврће свеже?	Are the vegetables fresh?
Ја желим један килограм.	I want one kilogram.
Ја желим пола килограма.	I want half a kilogram.
Ја желим два килограма.	I want 2 kilograms.
Ја желим само једно паковање воћа.	I only want one box of fruit.
Могу ли да изаберем воће?	Can I choose the fruit by myself?
То је превише.	This is too much.
То је премало.	This is too little.
Та јабука је трула.	This apple is rotten.
Не, хвала лепа.	No, thank you very much.
Воће је за колач.	The fruit is for a cake.

Поврће је за супу.	The vegetables are for a soup.
Молим вас само велике комаде.	Only big pieces, please.
Молим вас само мале комаде.	Only small pieces, please.
Могу ли да добијем само пола?	Can I only get half?
Ја немам кесицу.	I don´t have a bag.
Ја немам ситниш.	I have no change.

9. Leisure – Слободно време

Шта радиш у слободно време?	What do you do in your leisure?
Имаш ли много слободног времена?	Do you have much leisure?
Имаш ли хоби?	Do you have a hobby?
Који је твој хоби?	What kind of hobby do you have?
Да ли волиш фудбал?	Do you like soccer?
Да ли играш кошарку?	Do you play basketball?
Мој хоби је кување.	My hobby is cooking.

Моји хобији су књиге и читање.	My hobbies are books and reading.
Мој хоби је свирање.	My hobby is playing music.
Ја свирам кларив и гитару.	I play piano and guitar.
Ја волим дуге шетње.	I like long walks.
Ја волим природу.	I like nature.
Мој хоби је планинарење.	My hobby is mountain climbing.
Мој хоби је гледање филмова.	My hobby is watching movies.
Како често се бавиш твојим хобијем?	How often do you deal with your hobby?
Сваки дан.	Every day.
Сваки викенд.	Every weekend.
Не често, само понекад.	Not often, just sometimes.
Имаш ли времена за то?	Do you have time for that?
Не увек.	Not always.
За хоби имам увек времена.	I always have time for a hobby.
Волиш да идеш у биоскоп?	Do you like going to the movies?

Волиш оперу?	Do you like the opera?
Када имам времена, ја остајем код куће.	When I have time, I stay at home.
Ја волим да гледам телевизију.	I like watching TV.
Ја радо сликам и цртам .	I like painting and drawing.
Мој хоби је јога.	My hobby is yoga.
Мој хоби је скијање.	My hobby is skiing.
Мој хоби је хокеј.	My hobby is ice hockey.
Мој хоби је пливање.	My hobby is swimming.
Ја идем сваки викенд да пливам на базен.	I go to the swimming pool every weekend.
Мој хоби су путовања.	My hobby is travelling.
Ја волим да посећујем градове.	I like to visit cities.
Ја волим да посећујем далеке земље.	I like to visit distant countries.
Ја се бавим спортом.	I do sports.
Којим спортом се бавиш?	What kind of sport do you do?
Ја се бавим одбојком.	I play volleyball.

| Ја играм столни тенис. | I play table tennis. |
| Ја немам хоби. | I have no hobby. |

10. Personal description – Опис особе

Како изгеда твоја другарица?	What does your girlfriend look like?
Она је ниска и има смеђу косу.	She is small and has brown hair.
Како изгледа твој друг?	What does your friend look like?
Он је висок и има плаву косу.	He is tall and has blond hair.
Шта он носи?	What does he wear?
Он носи панталоне и кошуљу.	He wears pants and a shirt.
Она носи увек сукње и блузе.	She always wears skirts and blouses.
Какав је његов карактер?	What is his character like?
Он је симпатичан и драг.	He is sympathetic and kind.
Она је модерна и интересантна.	She is modern and interesting.
Он је веома гласан.	He is very loud.

Она је весела.	She is cheerful.
Мој колега је сада веома љут.	My colleague is very angry now.
Зашто је твој колега љут?	Why is your colleague angry?
Његова јакна је прљава.	His jacket is dirty.
Моја колегиница је тужна.	My colleague is sad.
Зашто је твоја колегиница тужна?	Why is your colleague sad?
Њена сукња је прљава.	Her skirt is dirty.
Какав је твој пас?	What does your dog look like?
Он је мали, млад и брз.	It´s small, young and fast.
Каква је твоја мачка?	What does your cat look like?
Она је дебела и спора.	It´s fat and slow.
Каква је твоја ташна?	What does your bag look like?
Она је велика и скупа.	It´s big and expensive.
Она је лоше јер је жедна.	She´s feeling bad because she´s thirsty.
Каква је његова кошуља?	What does his shirt look like?

Каква је њена сукња?	What does her skirt look like?
Какав је његов капут?	What does his coat look like?
Моја кожа је тамна, зар не?	My skin is tanned, isn´t it?
Он је лоше јер је гладан.	He´s feeling bad because he´s hungry.

11. Apartment description – Опис стана

О, како је ваш стан велик!	Oh, how big is your apartement!
Је ли ваш стан скуп?	Is your apartment expensive?
Стан је огроман, али није скуп.	The apartment is huge, but not expensive.
Ви имате среће са станом.	You are lucky with the apartment.
Ваша тераса је пространа.	Your terrace is spacious.
Дневна соба је модерна и угодна.	The living room is modern and comfortable
Спаваћа соба је минијатурна.	The bedroom is tiny.
Овде примате госте, зар не?	This is where you receive the guests, isn´t it?
Наш балкон је мали, али леп.	Our balcony is small but beautiful.

Имате и трпезарију?	Do you have a dining room also?
Не, нажалост немамо трпезарију.	No, unfortunately we do not have a dining room.
Наше купатило је једноставно и практично.	Our bathroom is simple and practical.
Њихов тоалет је мали, али чист и леп.	Your toilet is small but clean and beautiful.
Је ли ваш стан топао?	Is your apartment warm?
О да, стан је веома топао.	Oh yes, the apartment is very warm.
Да ли имате оставу?	Do you have a storage room?
Не, нажалост немамо оставу.	No, unfortunately, we don´t have a storage room.
Какав је солитер?	What is the building like?
Солитер је стар, али леп.	The building is old, but beautiful.
Какав је лифт?	What is the lift like?
Лифт ради.	The lift is in use.
Ми немамо лифт.	We don´t have an elevator.
Каква је улица?	What is the street like?
Улица је дугачка и гласна.	The street is long and loud.

12. In the evening – Увече

Куда идемо вечерас?	Where are we going tonight?
Вечерас идемо на вечеру.	Tonight, we are going to dinner.
Куда идемо у суботу?	Where are we going on Saturday?
У суботу идемо у град.	On Saturday we are going in the town.
Куда тачно?	Where exactly?
Идемо да вечерамо у ресторан.	We are going to the restaurant for dinner.
Куда идемо после?	Where are we going afterwards?
После идемо у кафану.	Afterwards we will go to a coffee house.
Шта славимо у суботу?	What are we celebrating on Saturday?
У суботу славимо рођендан.	On Saturday we celebrate my birthday.
Када се видимо?	When will I see you?
Видимо се у пола осам.	See you at 7:30 pm.
Куда идеш сутра?	Where are you going tomorrow?

Сутра идем у позориште.	Tomorrow I´m going to the theatre.
Куда идеш сутра увече?	Where are you going tomorrow night?
Сутра увече не идем никуда.	I´m not going anywhere tomorrow night.
Куда идеш прекосутра?	Where are you going the day after tomorrow?
Прекосутра имам састанак с Лелом.	The day after tomorrow I have a date with Lela.
Око колико часова се видимо?	At what time will I see you?
Видимо се око пет.	See you around 5 o´clock.
До када остајемо у клубу?	Until when do we stay at the club?
До поноћи.	Until midnight.
Шта желиш да радиш сутра увече?	What do you want to do tomorrow in the evening?
Сутра увече желим да гледам телевизију.	Tomorrow in the evening I want to watch TV.
Куда желиш да идеш у петак увече?	Where do you want to go on Friday evening?
У петак увече желим да идем на изложбу.	On Friday evening I want to go to the exhibition.
Куда идемо у недељу увече?	Where do we want to go on Sunday evening?
У недељу увече идемо у оперу.	On Sunday evening we are going to the opera.

13. Everyday life – Свакодневица

Када се будиш?	When do you wake up?
Ја се будим сваки дан око седам.	I wake up around 7 o´clock every day.
Шта доручкујеш?	What do you eat for breakfast?
Волим лаган доручак.	I like a light breakfast.
Ја не доручкујем.	I don´t eat breakfast.
Ја волим ујутро много да једем.	I like to eat a lot in the morning.
Шта радиш преподне?	What do you do in the morning?
Преподне радим.	I work in the morning.
Преподне сам на послу.	In the morning, I´m at work.
Када ручаш?	When do you eat lunch?
Обично ручам око дванаест.	I usually have lunch around noon.
Шта обично ручаш?	What do you usually eat for lunch?
Ја једем у кантини.	I eat in the canteen.
Ја једем код куће.	I eat at home.
Ја кувам код куће сваки дан.	I cook at home every day.
Ја не ручам јер касно доручкујем.	I don´t eat lunch because I have a late breakfast.

Шта радиш послеподне?	What do you do in the afternoon?
Послеподне сам на послу.	In the afternoon I am at work.
Послеподне сам код куће с децом.	In the afternoon I am at home with the children.
Послеподне се одмарам.	In the afternoon I rest.
Да ли се дуго одмараш?	Do you rest long?
Ја се кратко одмарам.	I rest a little.
Ја се не одмарам јер немам времена.	I don´t rest because I don´t have time.
Шта радиш увече?	What do you do in the evening?
Увече гледам телевизију.	In the evening I watch TV.
Увече читам новине.	I the evening I read the paper.
Увече читам књиге.	In the evening I read books.
Увече спремам стан.	In the evening I tidy the apartment.
Увече сам с децом.	In the evening I am with the children.
Када идеш да спаваш?	When do you go to bed?
Обично идем касно да спавам.	I usually go to bed late.
Обично идем рано да спавам.	I usually go to bed early.

14. My job – Мој посао

Где радиш?	Where do you work?
Шта си по занимању?	What is your profession?
Какав је твој посао?	What is your job like?
Мој посао је интересантан и угодан.	My job is interesting and pleasant.
Мој посао је напоран и тежак.	My job is exhausting and difficult.
Мој посао је лаган и једноставан.	My job is easy and simple.
Имаш ли шефа?	Do you have a boss?
Мој шеф је веома угодан.	My boss is very pleasant.
Ја немам шефа, ја радим самостално.	I don´t have a boss, I am self-employed.
Моји сарадници на послу су симпатични.	My colleagues at work are likeable.
Ја радим од девет до пет.	I work from 9 to 5.
Понекад радим прековремено.	I work overtime sometimes.
Како идеш на посао?	How do you get to work?

Идем пешке јер је мој биро близу.	I walk becuase my office is close by.
Ја не желим да мењам посао.	I don´t want to change my job.
Ја волим мој посао јер је забаван.	I like my job because it is entertaining.
Јеси сада на боловању?	Are you on sick leave now?
Да, имам грипу.	Yes, I have a flu.
Данас требам да завршим посао.	Today I am supposed to finish my work.
Имам много посла.	I have a lot to do.
Имам мало посла.	I have little to do.

Serbian Reader
Updated August 2023

Level A1 Beginners = Novice Low/Mid

Snežana Stefanović: IDEMO DALJE 1
paperback, e-book, audiobook, interactive e-book with audio

Snežana Stefanović: SERBIAN: Vocabulary Practice A1 to the Book "Idemo dalje 1"
paperback & e-book

Snežana Stefanović: SERBIAN: Simple Sentences 1
paperback, e-book, audiobook, interactive e-book with audio

Level A1 = Novice Mid/High

Snežana Stefanović: IDEMO DALJE 2
paperback, e-book, audiobook, interactive e-book with audio

Snežana Stefanović: SERBIAN: Simple Sentences 2
paperback & e-book

Snežana Stefanović: Trifun i mali fudbaleri – Short Story
paperback & e-book

Snežana Stefanović: Learn Serbian Cyrillic
paperback & e-book

Snežana Stefanović: SERBIAN: Small Travel Vocabulary
e-book

Level A2 = Intermediate Low

Snežana Stefanović: IDEMO DALJE 3
paperback & e-book

Snežana Stefanović: A2 Jokes and Anecdotes Part 1
paperback & e-book

Snežana Stefanović: A2 Jokes and Anecdotes Part 2
paperback & e-book

Level A2 – B1 = Intermediate Mid/High

Snežana Stefanović: IDEMO DALJE 4
paperback & e-book

Level C1 = Advanced High

Snežana Stefanović: Vreme – Short Stories
paperback & e-book

Please visit us!
www.serbian-reader.com

Milton Keynes UK
Ingram Content Group UK Ltd.
UKHW010711040923
428018UK00014B/878